50 Sweet and Savory Snack Heaven Recipes for Home

By: Kelly Johnson

Table of Contents

- Honey Mustard Pretzel Bites
- Chocolate-covered Strawberry Popcorn
- Caprese Skewers with Balsamic Glaze
- Cinnamon Sugar Apple Chips
- Spicy Sriracha Popcorn
- Mini Spinach and Feta Quiches
- Nutella-Stuffed Banana Muffins
- Parmesan Garlic Roasted Chickpeas
- Raspberry Cheesecake Bites
- Buffalo Cauliflower Bites
- Blueberry Lemon Scones
- Teriyaki Beef Jerky
- Avocado Toast with Cherry Tomatoes
- Maple Glazed Pecans
- Smoked Salmon and Cream Cheese Stuffed Mini Bagels
- Sweet Potato Fries with Chipotle Mayo
- Raspberry Almond Thumbprint Cookies
- Mediterranean Hummus Platter
- Cheddar and Chive Popovers
- Trail Mix Energy Bars
- Bacon-wrapped Dates with Goat Cheese
- Roasted Red Pepper and Feta Pinwheels
- Salted Caramel Popcorn
- Mini Caprese Salad Skewers
- Pesto and Sundried Tomato Palmiers
- Chocolate-Dipped Strawberries
- Spinach and Artichoke Dip
- Lemon Blueberry Muffins
- Spicy Cajun Popcorn Shrimp
- Cranberry and Goat Cheese Crostini
- Almond Joy Energy Bites
- Buffalo Chicken Dip
- Garlic Parmesan Popcorn
- Strawberry Shortcake Bites
- Jalapeño Poppers

- White Chocolate Macadamia Nut Cookies
- Prosciutto-wrapped Melon
- Cheesy Spinach and Artichoke Stuffed Mushrooms
- S'mores Popcorn Balls
- Mediterranean Stuffed Grape Leaves
- Peanut Butter and Banana Roll-ups
- Mini Margherita Pizzas
- Maple Bacon Popcorn
- Raspberry Chocolate Chip Muffins
- Teriyaki Chicken Wings
- Caramel Apple Nachos
- Herbed Goat Cheese and Roasted Tomato Crostini
- BBQ Sweet Potato Chips
- Mini Raspberry Tarts
- Spicy Guacamole with Homemade Tortilla Chips

Honey Mustard Pretzel Bites

Ingredients:

- 1 pound (about 4 cups) pretzel bites
- 1/2 cup unsalted butter, melted
- 1/4 cup Dijon mustard
- 1/4 cup honey
- 1 tablespoon yellow mustard
- 1 teaspoon garlic powder
- 1/2 teaspoon onion powder
- Salt, to taste (optional)

Instructions:

Preheat your oven to 350°F (175°C) and line a baking sheet with parchment paper.
In a small bowl, whisk together the melted butter, Dijon mustard, honey, yellow mustard, garlic powder, and onion powder until well combined.
Place the pretzel bites in a large mixing bowl.
Pour the honey mustard mixture over the pretzel bites, ensuring they are well coated. You can use a spatula or your hands to gently toss the pretzels, making sure each one is covered with the sauce.
Spread the coated pretzel bites evenly on the prepared baking sheet.
Optional: Sprinkle a bit of salt over the pretzel bites if you prefer a touch of saltiness.
Bake in the preheated oven for 10-12 minutes or until the pretzels are golden brown and slightly crispy.
Remove from the oven and let them cool for a few minutes before serving.
Enjoy your homemade honey mustard pretzel bites as a sweet and savory snack!

Chocolate-covered Strawberry Popcorn

Ingredients:

- 8 cups popped popcorn (about 1/2 cup unpopped kernels)
- 1 cup semi-sweet chocolate chips
- 1 cup white chocolate chips
- 1 cup freeze-dried strawberries, crushed
- 1 tablespoon vegetable oil
- Sprinkles (optional)

Instructions:

Pop the popcorn according to the package instructions. Make sure to remove any unpopped kernels and place the popped popcorn in a large mixing bowl.

In a heatproof bowl, melt the semi-sweet chocolate chips with 1/2 tablespoon of vegetable oil. You can do this in a microwave by heating in 20-second intervals, stirring in between until smooth. Alternatively, use a double boiler on the stovetop.

Drizzle the melted semi-sweet chocolate over the popped popcorn, ensuring even coverage. Toss the popcorn gently to coat it with the chocolate.

Spread the chocolate-coated popcorn on a parchment-lined baking sheet in a single layer.

In a separate bowl, melt the white chocolate chips with the remaining 1/2 tablespoon of vegetable oil using the same method as before.

Drizzle the melted white chocolate over the popcorn, creating a contrast with the semi-sweet chocolate. Use a spoon or spatula to create a marbled effect.

Immediately sprinkle the crushed freeze-dried strawberries over the chocolate-covered popcorn while the chocolate is still melted.

If desired, add colorful sprinkles for extra decoration.

Allow the chocolate-covered strawberry popcorn to cool and the chocolate to harden. You can speed up this process by placing the baking sheet in the refrigerator for about 15-20 minutes.

Once the chocolate is set, break the popcorn into clusters or bite-sized pieces.

Transfer the chocolate-covered strawberry popcorn to an airtight container or serve immediately.

Enjoy this delightful sweet and fruity chocolate-covered strawberry popcorn as a delicious snack!

Caprese Skewers with Balsamic Glaze

Ingredients:

- Cherry tomatoes
- Fresh mozzarella balls (small)
- Fresh basil leaves
- Balsamic glaze
- Olive oil (optional)
- Salt and pepper, to taste

Instructions:

Rinse the cherry tomatoes and fresh basil leaves. Drain any excess water.

On a clean surface, assemble your skewers. Take a skewer and slide on a cherry tomato, followed by a fresh basil leaf (folded, if large), and then a fresh mozzarella ball.

Repeat the pattern until the skewer is filled, leaving a little space at the end for easy handling.

Arrange the assembled Caprese skewers on a serving platter or tray.

Drizzle balsamic glaze over the skewers. If desired, you can also lightly drizzle with olive oil for added richness.

Sprinkle a pinch of salt and pepper over the skewers to taste.

Serve immediately as an elegant appetizer or party snack.

Enjoy the classic flavors of Caprese with the sweetness of tomatoes, creaminess of mozzarella, and the aromatic freshness of basil, all enhanced by the rich balsamic glaze!

Cinnamon Sugar Apple Chips

Ingredients:

- 3-4 large apples (preferably a sweet variety like Honeycrisp or Gala)
- 2 tablespoons granulated sugar
- 1 teaspoon ground cinnamon

Instructions:

Preheat your oven to 225°F (110°C). Line two baking sheets with parchment paper.

Wash and thinly slice the apples using a sharp knife or a mandolin. Aim for uniform thickness to ensure even baking.

In a small bowl, mix together the granulated sugar and ground cinnamon until well combined.

Place the apple slices in a large bowl and sprinkle the cinnamon-sugar mixture over them. Toss the apple slices gently to ensure they are evenly coated.

Arrange the coated apple slices in a single layer on the prepared baking sheets, making sure they do not overlap.

Bake in the preheated oven for 2-3 hours or until the apple chips are crisp and golden brown. Rotate the baking sheets halfway through the baking time for even cooking.

Keep an eye on the apple chips, as baking times may vary depending on the thickness of the slices and your specific oven.

Once the apple chips are done, remove them from the oven and allow them to cool on the baking sheets for a few minutes.

Transfer the cinnamon sugar apple chips to a wire rack to cool completely. They will continue to crisp up as they cool.

Store the apple chips in an airtight container at room temperature for up to a week. Enjoy this sweet and wholesome snack!

Spicy Sriracha Popcorn

Ingredients:

- 1/2 cup popcorn kernels
- 3 tablespoons unsalted butter
- 2 tablespoons Sriracha sauce
- 1 teaspoon garlic powder
- 1/2 teaspoon onion powder
- 1/2 teaspoon smoked paprika
- Salt, to taste

Instructions:

Pop the popcorn kernels using your preferred method (air popper, stovetop, or microwave). Make sure to remove any unpopped kernels.

In a small saucepan over low heat, melt the butter.

Stir in the Sriracha sauce, garlic powder, onion powder, and smoked paprika into the melted butter. Mix well until the ingredients are fully combined.

Place the popped popcorn in a large mixing bowl.

Drizzle the Sriracha butter mixture over the popcorn, ensuring even coverage. Use a spatula or your hands to gently toss the popcorn, making sure each kernel is coated with the spicy mixture.

Sprinkle salt over the popcorn to taste, giving it a savory contrast to the heat.

Optional: If you prefer an extra kick, you can add more Sriracha sauce or sprinkle additional smoked paprika.

Serve immediately and enjoy your Spicy Sriracha Popcorn as a bold and flavorful snack for movie nights or gatherings!

Mini Spinach and Feta Quiches

Ingredients:

- 1 sheet of puff pastry, thawed
- 1 cup fresh spinach, chopped
- 1/2 cup feta cheese, crumbled
- 1/4 cup grated Parmesan cheese
- 4 large eggs
- 1/2 cup milk or cream
- 1/4 teaspoon salt
- 1/4 teaspoon black pepper
- 1/4 teaspoon nutmeg (optional)

Instructions:

Preheat your oven to 375°F (190°C). Grease a mini muffin tin or line with mini muffin liners.

Roll out the thawed puff pastry on a floured surface. Use a round cookie cutter or a glass to cut out circles slightly larger than the mini muffin cups.

Gently press each pastry circle into the mini muffin cups, forming little pastry shells. Make sure to leave a slight overhang.

In a medium-sized bowl, whisk together the eggs, milk or cream, salt, pepper, and nutmeg (if using).

Place a small amount of chopped spinach into each pastry shell, followed by crumbled feta and grated Parmesan.

Pour the egg mixture over the spinach and cheese in each pastry shell, filling almost to the top.

Bake in the preheated oven for 12-15 minutes or until the quiches are set and the pastry is golden brown.

Allow the mini spinach and feta quiches to cool in the muffin tin for a few minutes before transferring them to a wire rack.

Serve warm as appetizers or snacks. These mini quiches can be enjoyed fresh out of the oven or at room temperature.

Enjoy the delightful combination of spinach and feta in these bite-sized quiches, perfect for parties or brunch gatherings!

Nutella-Stuffed Banana Muffins

Ingredients:

- 2 cups all-purpose flour
- 1 teaspoon baking powder
- 1 teaspoon baking soda
- 1/2 teaspoon salt
- 3 ripe bananas, mashed
- 1/2 cup unsalted butter, melted
- 1/2 cup granulated sugar
- 1/2 cup brown sugar, packed
- 2 large eggs
- 1 teaspoon vanilla extract
- 1/2 cup Nutella (or hazelnut spread of your choice)

Instructions:

Preheat your oven to 350°F (175°C). Line a muffin tin with paper liners or grease the cups.

In a medium bowl, whisk together the flour, baking powder, baking soda, and salt. Set aside.

In a large mixing bowl, combine the mashed bananas, melted butter, granulated sugar, brown sugar, eggs, and vanilla extract. Mix until well combined.

Add the dry ingredients to the banana mixture and stir until just combined. Be careful not to overmix; a few lumps are okay.

Fill each muffin cup with a small amount of batter, just enough to cover the bottom.

Spoon a dollop of Nutella (about 1 teaspoon) onto the center of each muffin cup.

Top the Nutella with more batter until the muffin cups are about 2/3 full.

Use a toothpick or skewer to gently swirl the Nutella into the batter, creating a marbled effect.

Bake in the preheated oven for 18-20 minutes or until a toothpick inserted into the center comes out clean or with a few moist crumbs.

Allow the Nutella-stuffed banana muffins to cool in the muffin tin for a few minutes before transferring them to a wire rack to cool completely.

Serve these delicious muffins as a delightful treat for breakfast or as a sweet snack.

Enjoy the combination of banana and Nutella in every bite!

Parmesan Garlic Roasted Chickpeas

Ingredients:

- 2 cans (15 ounces each) chickpeas (garbanzo beans), drained and rinsed
- 2 tablespoons olive oil
- 1/2 cup grated Parmesan cheese
- 2 teaspoons garlic powder
- 1 teaspoon onion powder
- 1 teaspoon dried oregano
- 1/2 teaspoon salt
- 1/4 teaspoon black pepper
- 1/4 teaspoon red pepper flakes (optional, for added heat)

Instructions:

Preheat your oven to 400°F (200°C). Line a baking sheet with parchment paper. Pat the chickpeas dry with a clean kitchen towel or paper towels to remove excess moisture.

In a large bowl, combine the chickpeas, olive oil, Parmesan cheese, garlic powder, onion powder, dried oregano, salt, black pepper, and red pepper flakes (if using). Toss until the chickpeas are evenly coated with the seasonings.

Spread the seasoned chickpeas in a single layer on the prepared baking sheet.

Bake in the preheated oven for 25-30 minutes or until the chickpeas are golden brown and crispy. Stir or shake the pan halfway through the baking time to ensure even cooking.

Remove the roasted chickpeas from the oven and let them cool on the baking sheet for a few minutes.

Transfer the Parmesan garlic roasted chickpeas to a serving bowl or enjoy them as a crunchy snack right off the baking sheet.

Allow any leftovers to cool completely before storing them in an airtight container.

These roasted chickpeas make a flavorful and protein-packed snack, perfect for munching on their own or as a topping for salads and soups. Enjoy!

Raspberry Cheesecake Bites

Ingredients:

- 1 cup graham cracker crumbs
- 3 tablespoons unsalted butter, melted
- 8 ounces cream cheese, softened
- 1/2 cup powdered sugar
- 1 teaspoon vanilla extract
- 1/2 cup fresh raspberries, plus extra for garnish
- 1/4 cup raspberry jam or preserves
- White chocolate chips or white chocolate melting wafers (optional, for drizzling)

Instructions:

In a medium bowl, combine the graham cracker crumbs and melted butter. Stir until the crumbs are evenly coated.

Press the graham cracker mixture firmly into the bottom of a square or rectangular baking dish to create a crust. Place the dish in the refrigerator while preparing the cheesecake filling.

In a mixing bowl, beat the softened cream cheese until smooth and creamy.

Add the powdered sugar and vanilla extract to the cream cheese, and continue to beat until well combined and smooth.

Gently fold in the fresh raspberries, being careful not to crush them completely.

Remove the prepared crust from the refrigerator and spread the cream cheese mixture evenly over the crust.

In a small saucepan, heat the raspberry jam over low heat until it becomes more liquid. Spoon small dollops of the jam over the cream cheese mixture.

Use a toothpick or a knife to swirl the raspberry jam into the cream cheese mixture, creating a marbled effect.

Place the dish back in the refrigerator and let it chill for at least 2 hours or until the cheesecake is firm.

Once chilled, use a sharp knife to cut the cheesecake into bite-sized squares.

Optional: Melt white chocolate chips or melting wafers according to package instructions. Drizzle the melted white chocolate over the raspberry cheesecake bites for added sweetness and decoration.

Garnish each square with a fresh raspberry on top.

Serve and enjoy these delicious raspberry cheesecake bites as a delightful dessert or a sweet treat for special occasions!

Buffalo Cauliflower Bites

Ingredients:

- 1 head of cauliflower, cut into florets
- 1 cup all-purpose flour
- 1 cup water
- 1 teaspoon garlic powder
- 1 teaspoon onion powder
- 1/2 teaspoon smoked paprika
- 1/2 teaspoon salt
- 1/4 teaspoon black pepper
- 1 cup buffalo sauce
- 2 tablespoons unsalted butter, melted
- Ranch or blue cheese dressing, for dipping

Instructions:

Preheat your oven to 450°F (230°C). Line a baking sheet with parchment paper.
In a large mixing bowl, whisk together the flour, water, garlic powder, onion powder, smoked paprika, salt, and black pepper to create a batter.
Dip each cauliflower floret into the batter, making sure it's fully coated, and then place it on the prepared baking sheet. Repeat until all cauliflower florets are coated.
Bake in the preheated oven for 20-25 minutes or until the cauliflower is golden brown and crispy.
While the cauliflower is baking, in a separate bowl, mix together the buffalo sauce and melted butter.
Once the cauliflower is done baking, remove it from the oven and carefully toss the florets in the buffalo sauce mixture until they are well coated.
Return the coated cauliflower to the baking sheet and bake for an additional 10-15 minutes, or until the sauce is sticky and the cauliflower has absorbed the flavors.
Remove from the oven and let the buffalo cauliflower bites cool slightly.
Serve the buffalo cauliflower bites with a side of ranch or blue cheese dressing for dipping.
Enjoy these spicy and flavorful buffalo cauliflower bites as a tasty appetizer or a game day snack!

Blueberry Lemon Scones

Ingredients:

- 2 cups all-purpose flour
- 1/2 cup granulated sugar
- 1 tablespoon baking powder
- 1/2 teaspoon salt
- 1/2 cup unsalted butter, cold and cut into small cubes
- 1 cup fresh blueberries
- Zest of 1 lemon
- 2/3 cup milk (whole milk or buttermilk)
- 1 large egg
- 1 teaspoon vanilla extract

For the Glaze:

- 1 cup powdered sugar
- 2 tablespoons fresh lemon juice
- Zest of 1 lemon

Instructions:

Preheat your oven to 400°F (200°C). Line a baking sheet with parchment paper.
In a large mixing bowl, whisk together the flour, sugar, baking powder, and salt.
Add the cold, cubed butter to the flour mixture. Use a pastry cutter or your fingers to cut the butter into the flour until the mixture resembles coarse crumbs.
Gently fold in the fresh blueberries and lemon zest until evenly distributed.
In a separate bowl, whisk together the milk, egg, and vanilla extract.
Pour the wet ingredients into the dry ingredients and stir until just combined. Be careful not to overmix; the dough should be slightly crumbly.
Turn the dough out onto a floured surface and gently knead it a few times to bring it together. Pat the dough into a circle about 1 inch thick.
Use a sharp knife or a round cookie cutter to cut the dough into scones. Place the scones on the prepared baking sheet, leaving some space between them.
Bake in the preheated oven for 15-18 minutes or until the scones are golden brown and cooked through.
While the scones are baking, prepare the glaze. In a bowl, whisk together the powdered sugar, fresh lemon juice, and lemon zest until smooth.

Once the scones are done baking, let them cool on the baking sheet for a few minutes before transferring them to a wire rack.

Drizzle the lemon glaze over the cooled scones.

Serve the blueberry lemon scones warm or at room temperature. Enjoy with a cup of tea or coffee!

These scones are a delightful combination of sweet blueberries and zesty lemon flavors.

Teriyaki Beef Jerky

Ingredients:

- 1 to 1.5 pounds beef sirloin or flank steak, thinly sliced against the grain
- 1/2 cup soy sauce
- 1/4 cup mirin (Japanese sweet rice wine)
- 2 tablespoons brown sugar
- 2 tablespoons honey
- 1 tablespoon rice vinegar
- 1 teaspoon garlic powder
- 1 teaspoon onion powder
- 1/2 teaspoon ground ginger
- 1/4 teaspoon black pepper
- Sesame seeds (optional, for garnish)

Instructions:

In a bowl, whisk together the soy sauce, mirin, brown sugar, honey, rice vinegar, garlic powder, onion powder, ground ginger, and black pepper to create the teriyaki marinade.

Place the thinly sliced beef into a resealable plastic bag or shallow dish.

Pour the teriyaki marinade over the beef, ensuring that all slices are well-coated.

Seal the bag or cover the dish and refrigerate for at least 4 hours, or preferably overnight, to allow the flavors to marinate.

Preheat your oven or dehydrator to the lowest setting (usually around 150°F or 65°C).

Remove the marinated beef from the refrigerator and let it come to room temperature for about 15-20 minutes.

If using an oven, place a wire rack on top of a baking sheet to allow air circulation. Arrange the marinated beef slices on the rack.

If using a dehydrator, arrange the beef slices on the dehydrator trays, leaving space between each slice.

Bake in the preheated oven or dehydrate according to your equipment's instructions until the beef jerky is dried and firm, usually 4-6 hours.

Check the beef jerky for doneness. It should be dry but still pliable. If it cracks and breaks when bent, it may be overcooked.

Optional: While the jerky is still warm, sprinkle sesame seeds over the top for added flavor and texture.

Allow the teriyaki beef jerky to cool completely before storing it in an airtight container.

Enjoy this homemade teriyaki beef jerky as a delicious and protein-packed snack!

Avocado Toast with Cherry Tomatoes

Ingredients:

- 2 slices of your favorite bread (sourdough, whole grain, or multigrain)
- 1 ripe avocado
- Cherry tomatoes, sliced
- Olive oil, for drizzling
- Salt and black pepper, to taste
- Red pepper flakes (optional, for added heat)
- Fresh cilantro or basil, chopped (optional, for garnish)
- Lemon wedges (optional, for serving)

Instructions:

Toast the slices of bread to your liking. You can use a toaster or toaster oven for this step.

While the bread is toasting, cut the ripe avocado in half, remove the pit, and scoop the flesh into a bowl. Mash the avocado with a fork until it reaches your desired consistency.

Once the bread is toasted, spread the mashed avocado evenly on each slice.

Arrange the sliced cherry tomatoes on top of the mashed avocado.

Drizzle olive oil over the avocado and tomatoes. The amount can be adjusted to your preference.

Season with salt and black pepper to taste. If you like a bit of heat, sprinkle red pepper flakes over the top.

Optional: Garnish with chopped cilantro or basil for added freshness and flavor.

Serve the avocado toast with cherry tomatoes immediately. If desired, squeeze a bit of fresh lemon juice over the top before enjoying.

This simple and delicious avocado toast with cherry tomatoes makes for a nutritious breakfast, brunch, or snack. Enjoy the creamy avocado paired with the burst of sweetness from the cherry tomatoes!

Maple Glazed Pecans

Ingredients:

- 2 cups pecan halves
- 1/4 cup pure maple syrup
- 2 tablespoons unsalted butter, melted
- 1/2 teaspoon vanilla extract
- 1/2 teaspoon ground cinnamon
- 1/4 teaspoon salt

Instructions:

Preheat your oven to 325°F (163°C). Line a baking sheet with parchment paper.
In a bowl, mix together the maple syrup, melted butter, vanilla extract, ground cinnamon, and salt.
Add the pecan halves to the maple syrup mixture, stirring well to ensure all the pecans are coated.
Spread the coated pecans in a single layer on the prepared baking sheet.
Bake in the preheated oven for 15-20 minutes, stirring the pecans halfway through the baking time. Keep a close eye on them to prevent burning.
Remove the pecans from the oven when they are golden brown and fragrant.
Allow the maple glazed pecans to cool on the baking sheet. As they cool, the glaze will harden and coat the pecans.
Once completely cooled, break the pecans apart if they've stuck together.
Store the maple glazed pecans in an airtight container at room temperature.
Enjoy these sweet and crunchy maple glazed pecans as a snack, salad topper, or as part of your favorite desserts!

Smoked Salmon and Cream Cheese Stuffed Mini Bagelso

Ingredients:

- Mini bagels (store-bought or homemade)
- 8 ounces smoked salmon, thinly sliced
- 4 ounces cream cheese, softened
- 1 tablespoon fresh dill, chopped
- 1 tablespoon capers, drained
- Red onion, thinly sliced (optional)
- Lemon wedges, for serving

Instructions:

Slice the mini bagels in half horizontally. If they are not pre-sliced, use a serrated knife to carefully cut them.

In a bowl, combine the softened cream cheese and chopped fresh dill. Mix well until the dill is evenly distributed throughout the cream cheese.

Spread a generous amount of the dill-infused cream cheese on the cut sides of each mini bagel half.

Lay a few slices of smoked salmon on the bottom half of each bagel.

Sprinkle capers over the smoked salmon. If desired, add thinly sliced red onion for extra flavor.

Place the top half of the bagel on the filling, creating a mini bagel sandwich.

Repeat the process for the remaining mini bagels.

Serve the smoked salmon and cream cheese stuffed mini bagels with lemon wedges on the side.

Arrange the mini bagels on a platter for a delightful brunch or breakfast spread. Enjoy these delicious and elegant mini bagel sandwiches as a tasty treat for any occasion!

Raspberry Almond Thumbprint Cookies
Ingredients:

- 1 cup unsalted butter, softened
- 2/3 cup granulated sugar
- 1/2 teaspoon almond extract
- 2 cups all-purpose flour
- 1/2 cup raspberry jam or preserves
- 1/2 cup almond flour (or finely ground almonds)
- Powdered sugar, for dusting (optional)

Instructions:

Preheat your oven to 350°F (175°C). Line a baking sheet with parchment paper.
In a large mixing bowl, cream together the softened butter, granulated sugar, and almond extract until light and fluffy.
Gradually add the all-purpose flour to the butter mixture, mixing until well combined. The dough should come together and be easy to handle.
Shape the dough into 1-inch balls and place them on the prepared baking sheet, spacing them about 2 inches apart.
Use your thumb or the back of a small spoon to make an indentation in the center of each cookie.
Fill each indentation with about 1/2 teaspoon of raspberry jam or preserves.
In a separate bowl, mix the almond flour (or finely ground almonds) until well combined.
Gently press the almond flour onto the exposed edges of the jam in each cookie, creating a decorative border.
Bake in the preheated oven for 12-15 minutes or until the edges of the cookies are lightly golden.
Allow the cookies to cool on the baking sheet for a few minutes before transferring them to a wire rack to cool completely.
Optional: Dust the cooled raspberry almond thumbprint cookies with powdered sugar for a finishing touch.
Serve and enjoy these delightful cookies with a cup of tea or coffee!

These raspberry almond thumbprint cookies are a perfect combination of buttery, nutty, and fruity flavors.

Mediterranean Hummus Platter

Ingredients:

For the Hummus:

- 2 cans (15 ounces each) chickpeas, drained and rinsed
- 1/3 cup tahini
- 2 cloves garlic, minced
- 1/4 cup extra virgin olive oil
- 1/4 cup fresh lemon juice
- 1 teaspoon ground cumin
- Salt, to taste
- Water (as needed for desired consistency)

For the Platter:

- Cherry tomatoes, halved
- Cucumber, sliced
- Kalamata olives
- Feta cheese, crumbled
- Red onion, thinly sliced
- Fresh parsley, chopped
- Extra virgin olive oil, for drizzling
- Pita bread or pita chips, for serving

Instructions:

In a food processor, combine the drained chickpeas, tahini, minced garlic, olive oil, lemon juice, ground cumin, and salt. Blend until smooth.

If the hummus is too thick, add water, one tablespoon at a time, until you achieve your desired consistency. Continue blending until smooth and creamy.

Taste the hummus and adjust the seasoning, adding more salt or lemon juice as needed.

Transfer the hummus to a serving bowl or arrange it on a platter.

Surround the hummus with cherry tomatoes, cucumber slices, Kalamata olives, crumbled feta cheese, thinly sliced red onion, and chopped fresh parsley.

Drizzle extra virgin olive oil over the hummus and the other elements on the platter.

Serve the Mediterranean hummus platter with pita bread or pita chips on the side.

Enjoy this flavorful and colorful spread as a delicious appetizer or snack for gatherings or parties!

Cheddar and Chive Popovers

Ingredients:

- 2 cups whole milk, at room temperature
- 4 large eggs, at room temperature
- 1/2 cup unsalted butter, melted
- 2 cups all-purpose flour
- 1 teaspoon salt
- 1 1/2 cups sharp cheddar cheese, shredded
- 3 tablespoons fresh chives, finely chopped

Instructions:

Preheat your oven to 425°F (220°C). Place a popover pan or muffin tin in the oven while it preheats.
In a blender or food processor, combine the milk, eggs, and melted butter. Blend until well combined.
In a large mixing bowl, whisk together the flour and salt.
Pour the wet ingredients from the blender into the dry ingredients. Whisk until just combined, avoiding overmixing. The batter will be thin.
Remove the hot popover pan or muffin tin from the oven. Grease the cups with a little butter or cooking spray.
Quickly pour the batter into the cups, filling each about halfway.
Sprinkle the shredded cheddar cheese and chopped chives over the batter in each cup.
Place the pan back in the oven and bake for 15 minutes.
Without opening the oven, reduce the temperature to 350°F (175°C) and continue baking for an additional 15-20 minutes or until the popovers are golden brown and puffed.
Once done, remove the popovers from the oven and serve immediately.
Enjoy these delicious cheddar and chive popovers as a savory accompaniment to meals or as a delightful snack!

Trail Mix Energy Bars

Ingredients:

- 1 cup old-fashioned rolled oats
- 1/2 cup unsalted almonds, chopped
- 1/2 cup unsalted walnuts, chopped
- 1/4 cup sunflower seeds
- 1/4 cup pumpkin seeds
- 1/4 cup shredded coconut
- 1/4 cup dried cranberries
- 1/4 cup raisins
- 1/4 cup mini chocolate chips (optional)
- 1/2 cup nut butter (almond butter, peanut butter, or your choice)
- 1/3 cup honey or maple syrup
- 1 teaspoon vanilla extract
- Pinch of salt

Instructions:

Preheat your oven to 350°F (175°C). Line a square baking dish with parchment paper, leaving an overhang for easy removal.

In a large mixing bowl, combine the rolled oats, chopped almonds, chopped walnuts, sunflower seeds, pumpkin seeds, shredded coconut, dried cranberries, raisins, and mini chocolate chips (if using). Mix well.

In a small saucepan over low heat, warm the nut butter, honey or maple syrup, vanilla extract, and a pinch of salt. Stir until the mixture is smooth and well combined.

Pour the wet ingredients over the dry ingredients in the bowl. Mix thoroughly until all the dry ingredients are coated.

Transfer the mixture to the prepared baking dish, pressing it down firmly and evenly.

Bake in the preheated oven for 15-20 minutes or until the edges turn golden brown.

Allow the bars to cool completely in the baking dish.

Once cooled, use the parchment paper overhang to lift the bars out of the dish. Place them on a cutting board and cut into desired-sized bars.

Store the trail mix energy bars in an airtight container at room temperature for up to a week, or refrigerate for longer shelf life.

Grab these homemade energy bars for a quick and nutritious snack on the go or during outdoor activities. Enjoy!

Bacon-wrapped Dates with Goat Cheese

Ingredients:

- Medjool dates, pitted
- Goat cheese, softened
- Almonds or pecans, whole or halves (optional)
- Bacon slices, cut in half
- Toothpicks

Instructions:

Preheat your oven to 375°F (190°C). Line a baking sheet with parchment paper.

If the dates are not pitted, carefully make a lengthwise slit in each date and remove the pit.

Stuff each date with a small amount of softened goat cheese. You can also add a whole or half almond or pecan inside the date.

Wrap each stuffed date with a half slice of bacon, making sure to cover the entire date. Secure with a toothpick through the center.

Place the bacon-wrapped dates on the prepared baking sheet, leaving space between each one.

Bake in the preheated oven for 15-20 minutes or until the bacon is crispy and golden.

Once cooked, remove the toothpicks from the bacon-wrapped dates.

Serve the bacon-wrapped dates with goat cheese as a delicious appetizer for parties, gatherings, or as a delightful sweet and savory treat.

Enjoy the combination of sweet dates, creamy goat cheese, and crispy bacon in every bite!

Roasted Red Pepper and Feta Pinwheels

Ingredients:

- 1 sheet puff pastry, thawed
- 1/2 cup roasted red peppers, finely chopped
- 1/2 cup crumbled feta cheese
- 1/4 cup fresh parsley, chopped
- 1 tablespoon olive oil
- 1 teaspoon dried oregano
- Salt and black pepper, to taste
- 1 egg (for egg wash)

Instructions:

Preheat your oven to 375°F (190°C). Line a baking sheet with parchment paper.
Roll out the thawed puff pastry on a lightly floured surface to smooth out any creases.
In a bowl, combine the chopped roasted red peppers, crumbled feta cheese, chopped fresh parsley, olive oil, dried oregano, salt, and black pepper. Mix well.
Spread the red pepper and feta mixture evenly over the puff pastry, leaving a small border around the edges.
Starting from one edge, carefully roll the puff pastry into a log or cylinder shape. Seal the edge by brushing it with a little water.
Place the puff pastry log in the refrigerator for about 15-20 minutes to firm up.
Once chilled, remove the log from the refrigerator and slice it into 1/2-inch thick pinwheels.
Place the pinwheels on the prepared baking sheet.
In a small bowl, beat the egg to create an egg wash. Brush the tops of the pinwheels with the egg wash.
Bake in the preheated oven for 15-18 minutes or until the pinwheels are golden brown and puffed.
Remove from the oven and let the pinwheels cool slightly before serving.
Serve these roasted red pepper and feta pinwheels as a delightful appetizer or snack. They can be enjoyed warm or at room temperature.
Enjoy the flavorful combination of roasted red peppers and tangy feta in these tasty pinwheels!

Salted Caramel Popcorn

Ingredients:

- 12 cups popped popcorn (about 1/2 cup unpopped kernels)
- 1 cup unsalted butter
- 1 cup brown sugar, packed
- 1/2 cup light corn syrup
- 1 teaspoon vanilla extract
- 1/2 teaspoon baking soda
- 1 teaspoon sea salt (adjust to taste)
- Optional: Flaky sea salt for additional garnish

Instructions:

Preheat your oven to 250°F (120°C). Line two large baking sheets with parchment paper or silicone baking mats.

Place the popped popcorn in a large mixing bowl, removing any unpopped kernels.

In a medium saucepan over medium heat, melt the butter. Stir in the brown sugar and corn syrup.

Bring the mixture to a boil, stirring constantly. Once it reaches a boil, let it cook without stirring for 4-5 minutes.

Remove the saucepan from heat and stir in the vanilla extract, baking soda, and sea salt. Be careful as the mixture will bubble up.

Pour the caramel sauce over the popped popcorn, stirring gently to coat the popcorn evenly.

Divide the caramel-coated popcorn between the prepared baking sheets, spreading it out into an even layer.

Bake in the preheated oven for 45-60 minutes, stirring every 15 minutes to ensure even coating.

Remove the caramel popcorn from the oven and let it cool completely on the baking sheets.

Once cooled, break the popcorn into clusters. If desired, sprinkle with additional flaky sea salt for a finishing touch.

Store the salted caramel popcorn in an airtight container to maintain its freshness.

Enjoy this sweet and salty treat as a snack for movie nights, parties, or any special occasion!

Mini Caprese Salad Skewers

Ingredients:

- Cherry tomatoes
- Fresh mozzarella balls (mini)
- Fresh basil leaves
- Balsamic glaze
- Extra virgin olive oil
- Salt and black pepper, to taste
- Toothpicks or small skewers

Instructions:

Rinse the cherry tomatoes and fresh basil leaves. Pat them dry with a paper towel.

On each toothpick or small skewer, thread a cherry tomato, followed by a fresh basil leaf, and then a mini mozzarella ball.

Arrange the mini Caprese salad skewers on a serving platter.

Drizzle balsamic glaze and extra virgin olive oil over the skewers.

Season with salt and black pepper to taste.

Serve immediately and enjoy these delightful mini Caprese salad skewers as a refreshing appetizer or snack for any occasion!

These skewers capture the classic Caprese flavors in a bite-sized and elegant presentation.

Pesto and Sundried Tomato Palmiers

Ingredients:

- 1 sheet puff pastry, thawed
- 1/2 cup pesto sauce (store-bought or homemade)
- 1/4 cup sundried tomatoes, finely chopped
- 1/2 cup grated Parmesan cheese
- Salt and black pepper, to taste
- Egg wash (1 egg beaten with 1 tablespoon water), for brushing

Instructions:

Preheat your oven to 375°F (190°C). Line a baking sheet with parchment paper.
On a lightly floured surface, roll out the thawed puff pastry to smooth out any creases.
Spread the pesto sauce evenly over the entire surface of the puff pastry.
Sprinkle the finely chopped sundried tomatoes and grated Parmesan cheese over the pesto layer.
Season with salt and black pepper to taste.
Starting from one edge, tightly roll the puff pastry into a log or cylinder shape.
Seal the edge by brushing it with a little water.
Place the puff pastry log in the refrigerator for about 15-20 minutes to firm up.
Once chilled, remove the log from the refrigerator and slice it into 1/2-inch thick palmiers.
Place the palmiers on the prepared baking sheet.
Brush the tops of the palmiers with the egg wash for a golden finish.
Bake in the preheated oven for 15-18 minutes or until the palmiers are golden brown and puffed.
Remove from the oven and let the palmiers cool slightly before serving.
Serve these pesto and sundried tomato palmiers as a delicious appetizer or snack. They can be enjoyed warm or at room temperature.
Enjoy the flavorful combination of pesto, sundried tomatoes, and Parmesan cheese in these delightful palmiers!

Chocolate-Dipped Strawberries

Ingredients:

- Fresh strawberries, washed and dried
- Dark chocolate, milk chocolate, or white chocolate (or a combination)
- Optional: Chopped nuts, shredded coconut, sprinkles, or other toppings

Instructions:

Line a baking sheet or tray with parchment paper.

In a heat-safe bowl, melt the chocolate in the microwave in 20-30 second intervals, stirring between each interval. Alternatively, you can melt the chocolate using a double boiler on the stovetop.

Hold each strawberry by the stem and dip it into the melted chocolate, swirling to coat it evenly. Allow any excess chocolate to drip back into the bowl.

If desired, roll the chocolate-dipped strawberry in chopped nuts, shredded coconut, sprinkles, or other toppings while the chocolate is still wet.

Place the dipped strawberries on the prepared parchment paper, making sure they are not touching each other.

Allow the chocolate-dipped strawberries to set at room temperature or, for quicker setting, place them in the refrigerator for about 15-30 minutes.

Once the chocolate is set, transfer the chocolate-dipped strawberries to a serving platter or store them in an airtight container in the refrigerator until ready to serve.

Enjoy these delicious chocolate-dipped strawberries as a sweet and elegant treat for special occasions or as a delightful dessert!

Spinach and Artichoke Dip

Ingredients:

- 1 (10-ounce) package frozen chopped spinach, thawed and drained
- 1 (14-ounce) can artichoke hearts, drained and chopped
- 1/2 cup mayonnaise
- 1/2 cup sour cream
- 1 cup grated Parmesan cheese
- 1 cup shredded mozzarella cheese
- 1 teaspoon minced garlic
- 1/2 teaspoon onion powder
- 1/4 teaspoon salt
- 1/4 teaspoon black pepper
- 1/4 teaspoon crushed red pepper flakes (optional)
- 1 tablespoon olive oil (for greasing the baking dish)

For Serving (optional):

- Tortilla chips, pita chips, sliced baguette, or fresh vegetable sticks

Instructions:

Preheat your oven to 375°F (190°C). Grease a baking dish with olive oil.
In a large mixing bowl, combine the drained chopped spinach, chopped artichoke hearts, mayonnaise, sour cream, grated Parmesan cheese, shredded mozzarella cheese, minced garlic, onion powder, salt, black pepper, and crushed red pepper flakes if using. Mix until well combined.
Transfer the mixture to the prepared baking dish, spreading it evenly.
Bake in the preheated oven for 25-30 minutes or until the dip is hot and bubbly, and the top is lightly browned.
Remove from the oven and let the spinach and artichoke dip cool for a few minutes before serving.
Stir the dip gently before serving to ensure an even consistency.
Serve the spinach and artichoke dip with tortilla chips, pita chips, sliced baguette, or fresh vegetable sticks.
Enjoy this creamy and flavorful spinach and artichoke dip as an appetizer for parties, gatherings, or game day!

Lemon Blueberry Muffins

Ingredients:

- 2 cups all-purpose flour
- 1 cup granulated sugar
- 1 tablespoon baking powder
- 1/2 teaspoon salt
- 1/2 cup unsalted butter, melted
- 2 large eggs
- 1 cup milk
- 1 teaspoon vanilla extract
- Zest of 1 lemon
- 2 tablespoons fresh lemon juice
- 1 1/2 cups fresh or frozen blueberries

For the Streusel Topping (optional):

- 1/4 cup all-purpose flour
- 2 tablespoons granulated sugar
- 2 tablespoons cold unsalted butter, cut into small pieces

Instructions:

Preheat your oven to 375°F (190°C). Line a muffin tin with paper liners or grease the muffin cups.

In a large mixing bowl, whisk together the flour, sugar, baking powder, and salt.

In a separate bowl, mix together the melted butter, eggs, milk, vanilla extract, lemon zest, and lemon juice.

Pour the wet ingredients into the dry ingredients and stir until just combined. Do not overmix; the batter should be lumpy.

Gently fold in the blueberries until evenly distributed in the batter.

Scoop the batter into the prepared muffin cups, filling each about two-thirds full.

If making the streusel topping, in a small bowl, combine the flour and sugar. Cut in the cold butter pieces until the mixture resembles coarse crumbs. Sprinkle the streusel over the muffin batter.

Bake in the preheated oven for 18-22 minutes or until a toothpick inserted into the center of a muffin comes out clean.

Allow the muffins to cool in the tin for a few minutes before transferring them to a wire rack to cool completely.

Enjoy these delightful lemon blueberry muffins as a delicious breakfast or snack!

Spicy Cajun Popcorn Shrimp

Ingredients:

For the Popcorn Shrimp:

- 1 pound medium-sized shrimp, peeled and deveined
- 1 cup buttermilk
- 1 cup all-purpose flour
- 1 cup cornmeal
- 1 tablespoon Cajun seasoning
- 1 teaspoon garlic powder
- 1 teaspoon onion powder
- 1/2 teaspoon cayenne pepper (adjust to taste)
- Salt and black pepper, to taste
- Vegetable oil, for frying

For the Spicy Cajun Dipping Sauce:

- 1/2 cup mayonnaise
- 2 tablespoons ketchup
- 1 tablespoon hot sauce (adjust to taste)
- 1 teaspoon Cajun seasoning
- 1 teaspoon lemon juice
- Salt and black pepper, to taste

Instructions:

In a bowl, combine the buttermilk, Cajun seasoning, garlic powder, onion powder, cayenne pepper, salt, and black pepper. Add the peeled and deveined shrimp to the buttermilk mixture, ensuring they are well-coated. Marinate for at least 30 minutes or refrigerate for up to 4 hours.

In a separate bowl, combine the flour and cornmeal. Season with salt and black pepper.

Heat vegetable oil in a deep fryer or large, deep skillet to 350°F (180°C).

Remove the shrimp from the buttermilk mixture, allowing excess liquid to drip off. Dredge each shrimp in the flour and cornmeal mixture, pressing gently to adhere the coating.

Fry the coated shrimp in batches for 2-3 minutes or until golden brown and crispy. Use a slotted spoon to remove them from the oil and place them on a paper towel-lined plate to drain any excess oil.

In a small bowl, mix together all the ingredients for the spicy Cajun dipping sauce until well combined.

Serve the spicy Cajun popcorn shrimp hot with the dipping sauce on the side. Enjoy these flavorful and crispy spicy Cajun popcorn shrimp as a tasty appetizer or snack!

Cranberry and Goat Cheese Crostini

Ingredients:

- Baguette or French bread, sliced into 1/2-inch thick rounds
- Olive oil, for brushing
- 4 ounces goat cheese, softened
- 1/2 cup dried cranberries
- Honey, for drizzling
- Fresh thyme leaves, for garnish (optional)
- Balsamic glaze, for drizzling (optional)

Instructions:

Preheat your oven to 375°F (190°C).
Place the baguette slices on a baking sheet and brush each side with olive oil.
Bake in the preheated oven for 8-10 minutes or until the bread is toasted and lightly golden. Remove from the oven and let them cool slightly.
Spread a generous amount of softened goat cheese on each toasted baguette round.
Sprinkle dried cranberries over the goat cheese, distributing them evenly.
Drizzle honey over the cranberries and goat cheese. If desired, you can also add a few fresh thyme leaves for garnish.
Optional: Drizzle balsamic glaze over the top for an extra layer of flavor.
Arrange the cranberry and goat cheese crostini on a serving platter.
Serve these delightful crostini as a festive appetizer for holiday gatherings or any special occasion.
Enjoy the combination of creamy goat cheese, sweet cranberries, and the hint of honey in each bite!

Almond Joy Energy Bites

Ingredients:

- 1 cup old-fashioned oats
- 1/2 cup almond butter
- 1/4 cup honey
- 1/4 cup unsweetened shredded coconut, plus extra for rolling
- 1/4 cup chopped almonds
- 1/4 cup mini chocolate chips
- 1 teaspoon vanilla extract
- Pinch of salt

Instructions:

In a large mixing bowl, combine the old-fashioned oats, almond butter, honey, shredded coconut, chopped almonds, mini chocolate chips, vanilla extract, and a pinch of salt.

Stir the ingredients together until well combined.

Place the mixture in the refrigerator for about 30 minutes to make it easier to handle.

After chilling, take small portions of the mixture and roll them into bite-sized balls.

Roll each energy bite in additional shredded coconut to coat the exterior.

Place the almond joy energy bites on a parchment-lined tray or plate.

Refrigerate the energy bites for at least an hour to allow them to firm up.

Once firm, transfer the energy bites to an airtight container and store them in the refrigerator.

Enjoy these almond joy energy bites as a delicious and nutritious snack. They're perfect for a quick energy boost or a sweet treat without the guilt!

Buffalo Chicken Dip

Ingredients:

- 2 cups shredded cooked chicken (rotisserie chicken works well)
- 1 package (8 ounces) cream cheese, softened
- 1/2 cup ranch dressing
- 1/2 cup hot sauce (such as Frank's RedHot)
- 1 cup shredded cheddar cheese
- 1/2 cup crumbled blue cheese (optional)
- 1/4 cup chopped green onions (optional)
- Tortilla chips, celery sticks, or carrot sticks for serving

Instructions:

Preheat your oven to 350°F (175°C).
In a mixing bowl, combine the shredded chicken, softened cream cheese, ranch dressing, hot sauce, shredded cheddar cheese, and crumbled blue cheese (if using). Mix well until all ingredients are evenly combined.
Transfer the mixture to a baking dish, spreading it out into an even layer.
Bake in the preheated oven for about 20-25 minutes or until the dip is hot and bubbly.
If desired, broil for an additional 2-3 minutes to achieve a golden brown top.
Remove the buffalo chicken dip from the oven and let it cool for a few minutes.
Sprinkle chopped green onions over the top (if using) for added freshness.
Serve the buffalo chicken dip with tortilla chips, celery sticks, or carrot sticks.
Enjoy this flavorful and spicy buffalo chicken dip as a crowd-pleasing appetizer for parties, game day, or any gathering!

Garlic Parmesan Popcorn

Ingredients:

- 1/2 cup popcorn kernels
- 3 tablespoons unsalted butter
- 2 tablespoons olive oil
- 3 cloves garlic, minced
- 1/2 cup grated Parmesan cheese
- 1 teaspoon garlic powder
- 1 teaspoon onion powder
- 1/2 teaspoon dried oregano
- Salt and black pepper, to taste
- Fresh parsley, chopped (optional, for garnish)

Instructions:

Pop the popcorn kernels using your preferred method (air popper, stovetop, or microwave). Place the popped popcorn in a large bowl, removing any unpopped kernels.

In a small saucepan, melt the butter over medium heat. Add the olive oil and minced garlic, sautéing for 1-2 minutes until the garlic is fragrant but not browned.

Pour the garlic and butter mixture over the popped popcorn, tossing to coat the popcorn evenly.

In a separate bowl, combine the grated Parmesan cheese, garlic powder, onion powder, dried oregano, salt, and black pepper. Mix well.

Sprinkle the Parmesan seasoning over the popcorn, tossing again to ensure the popcorn is well coated.

Optional: Garnish with chopped fresh parsley for added flavor and color.

Serve the garlic Parmesan popcorn immediately and enjoy as a flavorful and savory snack for movie nights or gatherings!

Strawberry Shortcake Bites

Ingredients:

For the Shortcakes:

- 1 1/2 cups all-purpose flour
- 1/4 cup granulated sugar
- 2 teaspoons baking powder
- 1/2 teaspoon salt
- 1/2 cup unsalted butter, cold and cut into small pieces
- 1/2 cup milk
- 1 teaspoon vanilla extract

For the Strawberry Filling:

- 1 pound fresh strawberries, hulled and diced
- 2 tablespoons granulated sugar
- 1 teaspoon lemon juice

For the Whipped Cream:

- 1 cup heavy cream
- 2 tablespoons powdered sugar
- 1 teaspoon vanilla extract

Instructions:

Preheat your oven to 425°F (220°C). Line a baking sheet with parchment paper.
In a large bowl, whisk together the flour, sugar, baking powder, and salt.
Add the cold, diced butter to the dry ingredients. Use a pastry cutter or your fingers to cut the butter into the flour until the mixture resembles coarse crumbs.
Pour in the milk and vanilla extract. Stir until just combined. Do not overmix; the dough should be slightly sticky.
Turn the dough out onto a floured surface. Pat it into a rectangle about 1/2-inch thick.
Use a round biscuit cutter to cut out shortcakes from the dough. Place them on the prepared baking sheet.

Bake in the preheated oven for 10-12 minutes or until the shortcakes are golden brown.

While the shortcakes are baking, prepare the strawberry filling. In a bowl, combine the diced strawberries, granulated sugar, and lemon juice. Toss to coat the strawberries and let them macerate while the shortcakes cool.

In a separate bowl, whip the heavy cream, powdered sugar, and vanilla extract until stiff peaks form.

Once the shortcakes have cooled, slice each one in half horizontally.

Spoon some macerated strawberries onto the bottom half of each shortcake.

Top with a dollop of whipped cream.

Place the other half of the shortcake on top.

Optional: Garnish with additional whipped cream and sliced strawberries.

Serve these strawberry shortcake bites as a delightful and sweet treat for dessert or a special occasion!

Jalapeño Poppers

Ingredients:

- 12 large jalapeño peppers
- 8 ounces cream cheese, softened
- 1 cup shredded cheddar or Monterey Jack cheese
- 1 teaspoon garlic powder
- 1 teaspoon onion powder
- 1/2 teaspoon smoked paprika
- 1/2 teaspoon cumin
- Salt and black pepper, to taste
- 12 slices bacon, cut in half
- Toothpicks

Instructions:

Preheat your oven to 375°F (190°C). Line a baking sheet with parchment paper.
Cut the jalapeño peppers in half lengthwise and remove the seeds and membranes. Use caution and consider wearing gloves to protect your hands from the heat.
In a bowl, mix together the softened cream cheese, shredded cheddar or Monterey Jack cheese, garlic powder, onion powder, smoked paprika, cumin, salt, and black pepper until well combined.
Spoon the cream cheese mixture into each jalapeño half, filling them evenly.
Wrap each cream cheese-filled jalapeño half with a half-slice of bacon. Secure the bacon with toothpicks.
Place the bacon-wrapped jalapeño poppers on the prepared baking sheet.
Bake in the preheated oven for 20-25 minutes or until the bacon is crispy and the jalapeños are tender.
Optional: Broil for an additional 2-3 minutes to achieve a more golden brown finish.
Remove the toothpicks before serving.
Serve these jalapeño poppers as a delicious and spicy appetizer for parties, game day, or any gathering!

Enjoy the combination of creamy cheese, smoky bacon, and spicy jalapeños in every bite.

White Chocolate Macadamia Nut Cookies
Ingredients:

- 1 cup (2 sticks) unsalted butter, softened
- 1 cup granulated sugar
- 1 cup light brown sugar, packed
- 2 large eggs
- 1 teaspoon vanilla extract
- 3 cups all-purpose flour
- 1 teaspoon baking soda
- 1/2 teaspoon baking powder
- 1/2 teaspoon salt
- 1 1/2 cups white chocolate chips
- 1 cup macadamia nuts, chopped

Instructions:

Preheat your oven to 350°F (175°C). Line baking sheets with parchment paper.
In a large mixing bowl, cream together the softened butter, granulated sugar, and brown sugar until light and fluffy.
Add the eggs one at a time, beating well after each addition. Mix in the vanilla extract.
In a separate bowl, whisk together the flour, baking soda, baking powder, and salt. Gradually add the dry ingredients to the wet ingredients, mixing until just combined.
Fold in the white chocolate chips and chopped macadamia nuts until evenly distributed throughout the dough.
Drop rounded tablespoons of cookie dough onto the prepared baking sheets, leaving some space between each cookie.
Bake in the preheated oven for 10-12 minutes or until the edges are lightly golden.
Allow the cookies to cool on the baking sheets for a few minutes before transferring them to a wire rack to cool completely.
Enjoy these delicious white chocolate macadamia nut cookies with a glass of milk or your favorite beverage!

These cookies are a delightful combination of sweet white chocolate and crunchy macadamia nuts, creating a perfect treat for any occasion.

Prosciutto-wrapped Melon

Ingredients:

- 1 medium-sized melon (cantaloupe, honeydew, or watermelon)
- 8-10 slices of prosciutto
- Fresh basil leaves (optional, for garnish)
- Balsamic glaze (optional, for drizzling)

Instructions:

Cut the melon in half and remove the seeds. Use a melon baller or cut the melon into bite-sized cubes.

Take a slice of prosciutto and wrap it around each melon cube or ball. You can secure the prosciutto with toothpicks if needed.

Repeat the process for the remaining melon pieces.

Optional: Arrange the prosciutto-wrapped melon on a serving platter and garnish with fresh basil leaves.

Optional: Drizzle balsamic glaze over the prosciutto-wrapped melon for an extra burst of flavor.

Serve immediately and enjoy this simple and elegant appetizer that combines the sweetness of melon with the savory goodness of prosciutto. Perfect for summer gatherings or as a light and refreshing snack!

Cheesy Spinach and Artichoke Stuffed Mushrooms

Ingredients:

- 20 large mushrooms, cleaned and stems removed
- 1 tablespoon olive oil
- 1 small onion, finely chopped
- 2 cloves garlic, minced
- 1 cup frozen chopped spinach, thawed and drained
- 1/2 cup canned artichoke hearts, drained and chopped
- 1 cup cream cheese, softened
- 1 cup shredded mozzarella cheese
- 1/2 cup grated Parmesan cheese
- Salt and black pepper, to taste
- Chopped fresh parsley, for garnish (optional)

Instructions:

Preheat your oven to 375°F (190°C). Line a baking sheet with parchment paper. Clean the mushrooms and remove the stems. Place the mushroom caps on the prepared baking sheet.

In a skillet, heat olive oil over medium heat. Add the chopped onion and sauté until softened.

Add the minced garlic to the skillet and sauté for an additional 1-2 minutes until fragrant.

Add the thawed and drained chopped spinach to the skillet, stirring until heated through.

Stir in the chopped artichoke hearts and continue cooking for 2-3 minutes.

In a large mixing bowl, combine the cream cheese, shredded mozzarella, and grated Parmesan. Add the spinach and artichoke mixture to the bowl and mix until well combined.

Season the mixture with salt and black pepper to taste.

Spoon the spinach and artichoke mixture into the mushroom caps, pressing it down slightly.

Bake in the preheated oven for 20-25 minutes or until the mushrooms are tender and the filling is bubbly and golden.

Optional: Garnish the stuffed mushrooms with chopped fresh parsley before serving.

Serve these cheesy spinach and artichoke stuffed mushrooms as a delicious appetizer for parties, gatherings, or any special occasion!

S'mores Popcorn Balls

Ingredients:

- 8 cups popped popcorn (about 1/3 cup unpopped kernels)
- 1 cup mini marshmallows
- 1 cup chocolate chips
- 1/2 cup graham cracker crumbs
- 1/4 cup unsalted butter
- 1/4 cup light corn syrup
- 1/2 teaspoon vanilla extract
- 1/4 teaspoon salt
- Additional graham cracker crumbs for coating (optional)

Instructions:

Pop the popcorn using your preferred method (air popper, stovetop, or microwave). Place the popped popcorn in a large mixing bowl, removing any unpopped kernels.

In a large saucepan, melt the butter over medium heat. Add the mini marshmallows and stir until completely melted and smooth.

Stir in the light corn syrup, vanilla extract, and salt, continuing to heat until well combined.

Remove the saucepan from the heat and pour the marshmallow mixture over the popped popcorn. Use a spatula to gently fold and coat the popcorn with the marshmallow mixture.

Add the chocolate chips and graham cracker crumbs to the popcorn mixture. Again, gently fold until the chocolate chips are distributed throughout the mixture.

Allow the mixture to cool slightly, making it easier to handle.

Grease your hands with a little butter or cooking spray, and shape the mixture into balls. You can make them as large or small as you prefer.

Optional: Roll each popcorn ball in additional graham cracker crumbs for a finishing touch.

Place the popcorn balls on a parchment-lined tray or in cupcake liners to set.

Allow the S'mores popcorn balls to cool completely before serving.

Enjoy these delicious and fun S'mores popcorn balls as a sweet treat for parties, movie nights, or any special occasion!

Mediterranean Stuffed Grape Leaves

Ingredients:

For the Grape Leaves:

- 1 jar (about 8 ounces) grape leaves in brine, drained and rinsed
- 2 cups cooked rice (preferably short-grain)
- 1/2 cup pine nuts, toasted
- 1/2 cup fresh parsley, finely chopped
- 1/4 cup fresh dill, finely chopped
- 1/4 cup fresh mint, finely chopped
- 1/4 cup extra-virgin olive oil
- 1/4 cup lemon juice
- Salt and black pepper, to taste

For the Filling:

- 1 cup crumbled feta cheese
- 1/2 cup Kalamata olives, pitted and chopped
- 1/2 cup sun-dried tomatoes, chopped

For Serving:

- Extra-virgin olive oil
- Lemon wedges

Instructions:

In a large bowl, combine the cooked rice, toasted pine nuts, chopped parsley, dill, mint, olive oil, and lemon juice. Mix well.

Season the rice mixture with salt and black pepper to taste.

Prepare the grape leaves by gently separating them and trimming any tough stems.

Place a grape leaf flat on a clean surface, shiny side down. Spoon a small amount of the rice mixture onto the center of the leaf.

Add a little of the feta cheese, chopped Kalamata olives, and sun-dried tomatoes on top of the rice mixture.

Fold the sides of the grape leaf over the filling, then roll it tightly from the bottom to the top, creating a compact roll.

Repeat the process with the remaining grape leaves and filling.

Arrange the stuffed grape leaves in a serving dish.

Drizzle extra-virgin olive oil over the stuffed grape leaves and squeeze fresh lemon juice on top.

Refrigerate the stuffed grape leaves for at least 1-2 hours before serving to allow the flavors to meld.

Serve the Mediterranean stuffed grape leaves chilled as a delicious appetizer or part of a mezze platter.

Enjoy the unique and flavorful combination of herbs, rice, feta, and olives in these Mediterranean stuffed grape leaves!

Peanut Butter and Banana Roll-ups

Ingredients:

- 4 whole wheat tortillas
- 1 cup creamy peanut butter
- 2 ripe bananas, peeled and sliced
- Honey, for drizzling (optional)
- Cinnamon, for sprinkling (optional)

Instructions:

Lay out the whole wheat tortillas on a clean and flat surface.
Spread an even layer of peanut butter over each tortilla.
Place banana slices along one edge of each tortilla.
Optional: Drizzle honey over the banana slices and sprinkle with a dash of cinnamon for added sweetness and flavor.
Roll up each tortilla tightly, starting from the edge with the banana slices.
Use a sharp knife to slice each rolled-up tortilla into bite-sized pieces.
Arrange the peanut butter and banana roll-ups on a serving plate.
Optional: Drizzle a little extra honey on top for a finishing touch.
Serve these delicious peanut butter and banana roll-ups as a quick and satisfying snack or a nutritious breakfast option.

Enjoy the combination of creamy peanut butter, sweet bananas, and optional honey in each bite!

Mini Margherita Pizzas

Ingredients:

- Mini pizza crusts or small tortillas
- 1 cup tomato sauce
- 1 1/2 cups fresh mozzarella cheese, sliced or shredded
- Cherry tomatoes, sliced
- Fresh basil leaves
- Olive oil
- Salt and black pepper, to taste

Instructions:

Preheat your oven to the temperature recommended for your pizza crusts.
Place the mini pizza crusts or small tortillas on a baking sheet.
Spread a layer of tomato sauce on each crust, leaving a small border around the edges.
Arrange the fresh mozzarella slices or shredded mozzarella evenly over the tomato sauce.
Place sliced cherry tomatoes on top of the mozzarella.
Drizzle a little olive oil over each mini pizza for added flavor.
Season with salt and black pepper to taste.
Bake in the preheated oven according to the instructions for your pizza crusts or until the cheese is melted and bubbly.
Remove from the oven and garnish each mini Margherita pizza with fresh basil leaves.
Serve these mini Margherita pizzas hot as a delightful appetizer, snack, or party treat.

Enjoy the classic flavors of Margherita pizza in a bite-sized form!

Maple Bacon Popcorn

Ingredients:

- 8 cups popped popcorn (about 1/3 cup unpopped kernels)
- 6 slices bacon, cooked and crumbled
- 1/2 cup unsalted butter
- 1/2 cup pure maple syrup
- 1/4 cup brown sugar
- 1/2 teaspoon vanilla extract
- 1/4 teaspoon salt
- Optional: 1 cup chopped pecans or nuts of your choice

Instructions:

Preheat your oven to 300°F (150°C). Line a large baking sheet with parchment paper.
Place the popped popcorn in a large mixing bowl, removing any unpopped kernels. Add the crumbled bacon to the popcorn.
In a saucepan over medium heat, melt the butter. Stir in the maple syrup and brown sugar.
Bring the mixture to a gentle boil, stirring constantly. Allow it to boil for 4-5 minutes without stirring.
Remove the saucepan from the heat and stir in the vanilla extract and salt.
Pour the maple-butter mixture over the popcorn and bacon, tossing gently to coat evenly.
Optional: Add chopped pecans or your favorite nuts to the popcorn mixture and toss again.
Spread the maple bacon popcorn evenly on the prepared baking sheet.
Bake in the preheated oven for 20-25 minutes, stirring every 10 minutes to ensure even coating.
Remove the popcorn from the oven and let it cool completely on the baking sheet.
Once cooled, break the maple bacon popcorn into clusters.
Serve and enjoy this sweet and savory treat with the delightful combination of maple syrup and bacon!

Maple bacon popcorn is a delicious snack that combines the richness of maple syrup with the savory goodness of bacon for a perfect balance of flavors.

Raspberry Chocolate Chip Muffins

Ingredients:

- 2 cups all-purpose flour
- 1/2 cup granulated sugar
- 1/4 cup brown sugar, packed
- 1 teaspoon baking powder
- 1/2 teaspoon baking soda
- 1/4 teaspoon salt
- 1 cup buttermilk
- 1/2 cup unsalted butter, melted and cooled
- 2 large eggs
- 1 teaspoon vanilla extract
- 1 cup fresh or frozen raspberries
- 1/2 cup chocolate chips (dark, milk, or semi-sweet)

Instructions:

Preheat your oven to 375°F (190°C). Line a muffin tin with paper liners or grease the muffin cups.

In a large mixing bowl, whisk together the flour, granulated sugar, brown sugar, baking powder, baking soda, and salt.

In a separate bowl, whisk together the buttermilk, melted butter, eggs, and vanilla extract.

Pour the wet ingredients into the dry ingredients and stir until just combined. Do not overmix; the batter should be lumpy.

Gently fold in the raspberries and chocolate chips until evenly distributed in the batter.

Scoop the batter into the prepared muffin cups, filling each about two-thirds full.

Bake in the preheated oven for 18-22 minutes or until a toothpick inserted into the center of a muffin comes out clean.

Allow the muffins to cool in the tin for a few minutes before transferring them to a wire rack to cool completely.

Enjoy these delightful raspberry chocolate chip muffins as a delicious breakfast or snack!

The combination of sweet raspberries and chocolate chips makes these muffins a tasty treat for any time of the day.

Teriyaki Chicken Wings

Ingredients:

For the Teriyaki Sauce:

- 1/2 cup soy sauce
- 1/4 cup water
- 3 tablespoons brown sugar
- 2 tablespoons honey
- 1 tablespoon rice vinegar
- 1 teaspoon sesame oil
- 1 teaspoon minced garlic
- 1 teaspoon minced ginger
- 1 tablespoon cornstarch (optional, for thickening)

For the Chicken Wings:

- 2 pounds chicken wings, split at joints, tips discarded
- Salt and black pepper, to taste
- 2 tablespoons vegetable oil
- Sesame seeds and chopped green onions for garnish (optional)

Instructions:

Preheat your oven to 400°F (200°C). Line a baking sheet with parchment paper.
Pat the chicken wings dry with paper towels and season them with salt and black pepper.
In a bowl, whisk together the soy sauce, water, brown sugar, honey, rice vinegar, sesame oil, minced garlic, and minced ginger. If you prefer a thicker sauce, mix in the cornstarch.
Heat vegetable oil in a large skillet over medium-high heat. Add the chicken wings and cook until browned on all sides, about 5-7 minutes.
Transfer the browned chicken wings to the prepared baking sheet.
Brush the chicken wings with a generous amount of the teriyaki sauce.
Bake in the preheated oven for 35-40 minutes or until the chicken wings are cooked through and have a crispy exterior.
Optional: While baking, baste the wings with additional teriyaki sauce every 10-15 minutes for extra flavor.
Remove the wings from the oven and brush with more teriyaki sauce.

Garnish with sesame seeds and chopped green onions if desired.
Serve the teriyaki chicken wings hot as an appetizer or main dish.

Enjoy the sweet and savory flavor of these delicious teriyaki chicken wings!

Caramel Apple Nachos

Ingredients:

- 3-4 large apples, cored and sliced
- 1 cup caramel sauce
- 1/2 cup chopped nuts (pecans or walnuts), optional
- 1/2 cup mini chocolate chips
- 1/4 cup shredded coconut, optional
- 1/4 cup sprinkles, optional
- Whipped cream or vanilla ice cream for serving, optional

Instructions:

Arrange the sliced apples on a serving platter or individual plates, slightly overlapping.

Warm the caramel sauce in the microwave or on the stovetop according to the package instructions. Drizzle the warm caramel sauce generously over the sliced apples.

Sprinkle the chopped nuts, mini chocolate chips, shredded coconut, and sprinkles over the caramel-covered apples.

Optional: Add a dollop of whipped cream or a scoop of vanilla ice cream to the center of the apple nachos.

Serve the caramel apple nachos immediately, and enjoy this delightful and shareable dessert!

These caramel apple nachos are a fun and delicious way to enjoy the classic combination of caramel and apples with the added crunch of nuts and sweetness of chocolate chips.

Herbed Goat Cheese and Roasted Tomato Crostini

Ingredients:

- Baguette or French bread, sliced into 1/2-inch thick rounds
- 8 ounces goat cheese, softened
- 1 tablespoon fresh basil, chopped
- 1 tablespoon fresh thyme leaves
- 1 tablespoon fresh chives, chopped
- 2 cups cherry tomatoes, halved
- Olive oil
- Salt and black pepper, to taste
- Balsamic glaze, for drizzling (optional)

Instructions:

Preheat your oven to 400°F (200°C).

Place the sliced baguette rounds on a baking sheet. Drizzle olive oil over each slice and toast in the preheated oven for about 5-7 minutes or until they are golden brown.

In a bowl, mix together the softened goat cheese, chopped basil, thyme leaves, and chives until well combined.

In another bowl, toss the halved cherry tomatoes with olive oil, salt, and black pepper.

Heat a skillet over medium-high heat. Add the cherry tomatoes and cook for 3-5 minutes, or until they start to blister and release their juices. Remove from heat.

Spread a generous layer of the herbed goat cheese onto each toasted baguette round.

Top the goat cheese with the roasted cherry tomatoes.

Optional: Drizzle balsamic glaze over the crostini for an extra burst of flavor.

Arrange the herbed goat cheese and roasted tomato crostini on a serving platter.

Serve immediately as a delicious appetizer for parties or as a flavorful snack.

These crostini are a delightful combination of creamy goat cheese, fresh herbs, and sweet roasted tomatoes on crispy bread.

BBQ Sweet Potato Chips

Ingredients:

- 2 large sweet potatoes, peeled
- 2 tablespoons olive oil
- 1 teaspoon smoked paprika
- 1 teaspoon garlic powder
- 1/2 teaspoon onion powder
- 1/2 teaspoon cayenne pepper (adjust to taste)
- Salt and black pepper, to taste
- 1/4 cup barbecue sauce (plus extra for dipping, if desired)

Instructions:

Preheat your oven to 400°F (200°C). Line two baking sheets with parchment paper.

Using a mandoline slicer or a sharp knife, thinly slice the peeled sweet potatoes into rounds.

In a large bowl, toss the sweet potato slices with olive oil, smoked paprika, garlic powder, onion powder, cayenne pepper, salt, and black pepper until evenly coated. Spread the sweet potato slices.

Mini Raspberry Tarts

Ingredients:

For the Tart Shells:

- 1 1/4 cups all-purpose flour
- 1/4 cup granulated sugar
- 1/2 cup unsalted butter, cold and cubed
- 1 large egg yolk
- 2 tablespoons ice water

For the Raspberry Filling:

- 1 cup fresh raspberries
- 2 tablespoons raspberry jam or preserves

For the Cream Cheese Filling:

- 4 ounces cream cheese, softened
- 1/4 cup powdered sugar
- 1/2 teaspoon vanilla extract

Instructions:

In a food processor, combine the flour and granulated sugar. Add the cold, cubed butter and pulse until the mixture resembles coarse crumbs.

In a small bowl, whisk together the egg yolk and ice water. With the food processor running, gradually add the egg mixture until the dough comes together. Turn the dough out onto a floured surface and knead it a few times to bring it together. Shape the dough into a disk, wrap it in plastic wrap, and refrigerate for at least 30 minutes.

Preheat your oven to 375°F (190°C). Grease a mini tart pan.

Roll out the chilled dough on a floured surface to about 1/8-inch thickness. Cut out circles using a round cookie cutter that fits the size of your mini tart pan. Press the circles into the tart pan to form the shells.

Prick the bottom of the tart shells with a fork. Place a piece of parchment paper over each shell and fill it with pie weights or dry beans.

Bake the tart shells in the preheated oven for 10 minutes. Remove the weights and parchment paper, and bake for an additional 5-7 minutes or until the shells are golden brown. Allow them to cool completely.

In a small saucepan, heat the raspberry jam over low heat until melted. Remove from heat and let it cool slightly.

In a mixing bowl, beat together the softened cream cheese, powdered sugar, and vanilla extract until smooth.

Spread a small amount of the cream cheese filling into the bottom of each tart shell.

Arrange fresh raspberries on top of the cream cheese filling.

Brush the melted raspberry jam over the raspberries for a shiny glaze.

Refrigerate the mini raspberry tarts for at least 30 minutes before serving.

Serve these delightful mini raspberry tarts as a sweet and elegant dessert for any occasion!

Spicy Guacamole with Homemade Tortilla Chips

Ingredients:

For the Spicy Guacamole:

- 3 ripe avocados, peeled and pitted
- 1 small red onion, finely diced
- 1-2 jalapeños, seeds removed and finely diced
- 2 cloves garlic, minced
- 1/4 cup fresh cilantro, chopped
- Juice of 2 limes
- Salt and black pepper, to taste

For the Homemade Tortilla Chips:

- 8 small corn tortillas
- Olive oil
- Salt

Instructions:

Spicy Guacamole:

In a large bowl, mash the ripe avocados with a fork or potato masher until you achieve your desired level of smoothness.
Add the finely diced red onion, jalapeños, minced garlic, and chopped cilantro to the mashed avocados.
Squeeze the juice of 2 limes into the bowl.
Season the guacamole with salt and black pepper to taste.
Gently mix all the ingredients together until well combined.
Optional: Adjust the spice level by adding more jalapeños if desired.
Cover the guacamole with plastic wrap, ensuring the wrap is in direct contact with the surface of the guacamole to prevent browning. Refrigerate until ready to serve.

Homemade Tortilla Chips:

Preheat your oven to 350°F (175°C).

Brush each corn tortilla lightly with olive oil on both sides.
Stack the tortillas and cut them into wedges or desired chip size.
Arrange the tortilla wedges in a single layer on a baking sheet.
Sprinkle the tortillas with a little salt.
Bake in the preheated oven for 10-12 minutes or until the tortilla chips are crisp and golden brown.
Allow the tortilla chips to cool before serving.

Serving:

Serve the spicy guacamole in a bowl, garnished with additional cilantro if desired.
Arrange the homemade tortilla chips around the guacamole for dipping.
Enjoy this delicious and flavorful spicy guacamole with homemade tortilla chips as a perfect snack or appetizer!

www.ingramcontent.com/pod-product-compliance
Lightning Source LLC
LaVergne TN
LVHW081319060526
838201LV00055B/2355